CONTENTS

THE FIGHTING SHIP CLOSEUP   4
How it works

BIG BATTLESHIPS   6
Battling behemoths

MAJOR WARSHIPS   10
Modern marine menaces

SMALL WARSHIPS   12
Little but lethal

AIRCRAFT CARRIERS   16
Runways of the sea

DESTROYERS AND FRIGATES   18
Surface strike force

AMPHIBIOUS WARFARE VESSELS   24
Sea and landlubbers

LOGISTIC SUPPORT VESSELS   26
Lending a hand

SUBMARINES   28
Threats of the depths

GLOSSARY   30

INDEX   32

THE FIGHTING SHIP CLOSEUP

Warship technology changed little until the late 19th century, when steam power and iron armour made ships faster, stronger and more reliable. The first military ships were troop carriers, but today's vessels carry the latest weapons. Modern warships can even launch air attacks over vast distances. On the following pages you can read about some of the most powerful ships on the sea.

MEGA FACT
Iron warships first appeared in North America in the 19th century. They were powered by steam engines, so the crew no longer needed to rely on the wind to carry them along.

MEGA TOUGH
The first iron warships looked like floating castles, with armoured hulls and tall gun turrets.

PEAK PERFORMANCE
There are many different warship and submarine classes in service in the world's navies today, each with the latest hydrodynamics, propulsion systems and weaponry. Improvements in the on-board electronic equipment, for example, has improved dramatically in the last 30 years.

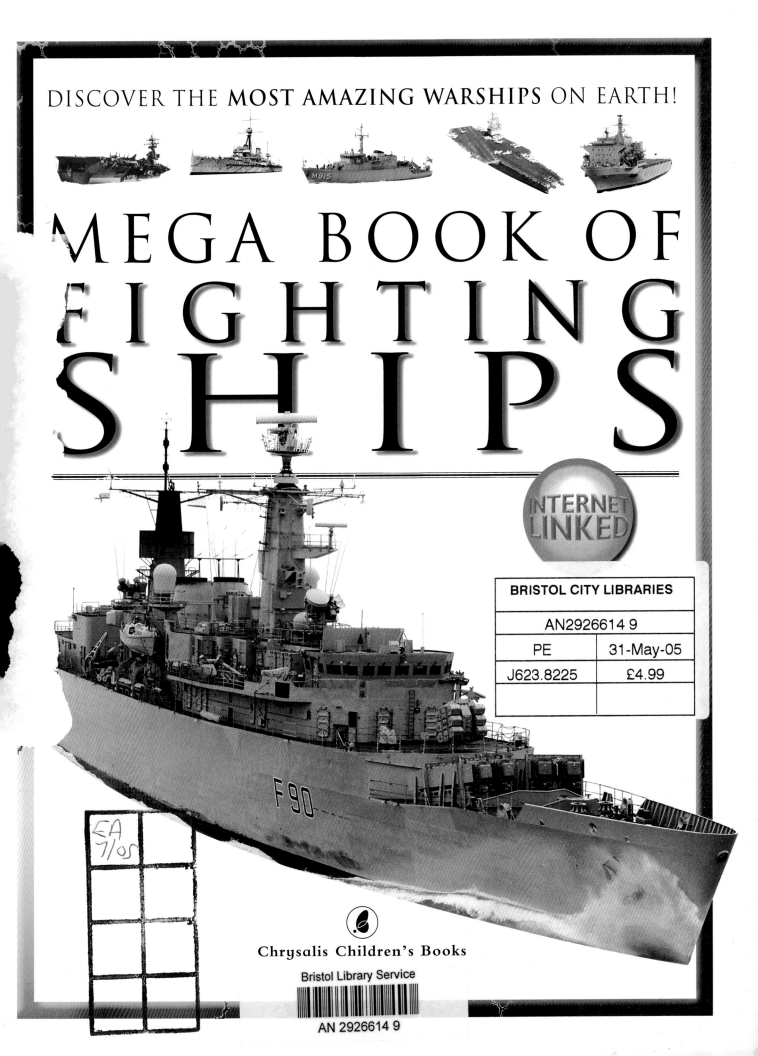

DISCOVER THE **MOST AMAZING WARSHIPS** ON EARTH!

MEGA BOOK OF FIGHTING SHIPS

INTERNET LINKED

F90

Chrysalis Children's Books

INTERNET LINKS

http://www.chinfo.navy.mil/navpalib/ships

This online guide includes images and technical specifications of some of the US Navy's most feared fighting ships.

http://www.fas.org/man

The website of the Federation of American Scientists provides links to military warships used by all the world's major naval forces.

http://www.hazegray.org

This website presents a range of statistics about modern warships, with regularly updated fleet lists.

http://www.naval-history.net

An excellent online resource with details of the naval battles of both World Wars, campaign summaries and much more.

http://www.navalhistory.plus.com

Find out about the naval conflicts during the 1982 Falklands War between Argentina and Britain. You can also flick through an impressive picture gallery of warships involved in the campaign.

http://www.royal-navy.mod.uk

Think you've got what it takes to serve in the navy? Find out at the official website of Britain's Royal Navy. This site includes a detailed history of this revered naval force and lots of information about its current military operations worldwide.

http://www.warships1.com

Statistics, hundreds of images and the histories of the world's main naval forces, including detailed technical specifications for many warships, past and present.

INTERNET SAFETY

Always follow these guidelines for a fun and safe journey through cyberspace:

1. Ask your parents for permission before you go online.

2. Spend time with your parents online and show them your favourite sites.

3. Post your family's e-mail address, even if you have your own (only give your personal address to someone you trust).

4. Do not reply to e-mails if you feel they are strange or upsetting.

5. Do not use your real surname while you are online.

6. Never arrange to meet 'cyber friends' in person without your parents' permission.

7. Never give out your password.

8. Never give out your home address or telephone number.

9. Do not send scanned pictures of yourself unless your parents approve.

10. Leave a website straight away if you find something that is offensive or upsetting. Talk to your parents about it.

Every effort has been made to ensure none of the recommended websites in this book are linked to inappropriate material. However, due to the ever-changing nature of the Internet, the publishers regret they cannot take responsibility for future content of these websites. Therefore, it is strongly advised that children and parents consider the safety guidelines above.

First published in the UK in 2003 by Chrysalis Children's Books
an imprint of Chrysalis Books Group Plc
The Chrysalis Building, Bramley Road, London, W10 6SP
This paperback edition first published in 2005
www.chrysalisbooks.co.uk
Copyright © Chrysalis Children's Books 2003

Editorial Director: Honor Head
Art Director: Sophie Wilkins
Senior Editor: Rasha Elsaeed
Project Editor: Leon Gray
Designer: Scott Gibson
Picture Researcher: Terry Forshaw

A CIP catalogue record for this book is available from the British Library.

ISBN 1 904516 10 6 (hb)
ISBN 1 84458 398 8 (pb)

Printed and bound in China.

This book can be ordered direct from the publisher.
Please contact the Marketing Department. But try your bookshop first.

Floating Arsenal

The Italian *Vittorio Veneto* (shown in the main picture and in outline below) remains a capable component of NATO's Mediterranean fleet, boasting a substantial weapons store and sophisticated electronics. This light aircraft carrier also has room for up to six Augusta-Bell AB 212 anti-submarine warfare (ASW) helicopters, each armed with homing torpedoes and air-to-surface missiles (ASM). It's truly a fearsome floating fighter!

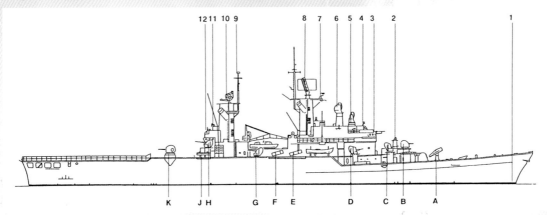

A	Mk 20 Mod 7 Aster launch system	1	SQS-23G hull-mounted sonar
B	Breda 40mm gun of Dardo CIWS	2	Selenia RTN-20X fire-control radar
C	76mm OTO Melara dual-purpose gun	3	SMA 3RM7 surface-search radar
D	76mm OTO Melara dual-purpose gun	4	Selenia RTN-10X fire-control radar
E	OTO Melara Otomat MkII launcher	5	SPG-55C SAM control radar
F	OTO Melara Otomat MkII launcher	6	SPG-55C SAM control radar
G	76mm OTO Melara dual-purpose gun	7	MM/SPS-768v1 target designator
H	76mm OTO Melara dual-purpose gun	8	Hughes SPS-52C long-range radar
J	324mm ILAS-3 ASW torpedo tubes	9	URN-20A Tacan antenna
K	Breda 40mm gun of Dardo CIWS	10	RAN-20X air-search radar
		11	Selenia RTN-10X fire-control radar
		12	Selenia RTN-20X fire-control radar

MEGA BATTLE

Germany lost so many ships during the 1916 Battle of Jutland in World War I (1914—1918) that the entire fleet remained in port for the rest of the war.

BIG BATTLESHIPS

By the turn of the 20th century, the world's major navies included some of the biggest battleships ever, such as Royal Navy's HMS *Dreadnought*. The onset of World War II (1939–1945) prompted even more ambitious vessels. Germany had the *Bismarck*, while Japan came up with the *Yamato* and *Musashi* – the largest and most heavily protected ships of their class in the world. Today, the title of 'capital ships' has passed on to the mighty aircraft carriers, such as the USS *Nimitz*, and nuclear-powered submarines armed with ballistic missiles.

MEGA LARGE!
At 52,832 tonnes, the Bismarck *was one of the largest German ships of World War II. But shortly after her launch, in 1941, she was sunk by the British Royal Navy.*

GUNS BLAZING
Bismarck and *Tirpitz* were the only battleships completed under the Nazi regime. These impressive vessels had a powerful primary armament of eight 380mm guns in four twin turrets. They also had extremely good air-defence weapons.

MEGA FORCES
Three US armed services operate on the world's oceans: the Navy, the Marine Corps and the Coast Guard.

Roman Ships

Although the ancient Greeks were the first to develop oar-driven warships, called triremes, the Romans copied and improved the designs, building them using heavier timbers and often adding an extra mast. The Romans also made the hinges to the boarding bridges much stronger and added a sharp spike that pinned the bridge to the deck of an enemy ship. Hundreds of galley slaves rowed the vessel, keeping time to a beating drum.

THE BATTLE OF DENMARK STRAIT

Apart from the ship's enormous weight, one of the most significant characteristics of the German battleship *Bismarck* (shown below) was her ability to withstand damage. The design of the ship's armour meant she was very well defended. Armed, too, with powerful 38cm guns, *Bismarck* looked invincible. But she set sail on her only operational voyage, accompanied by the heavy cruiser *Prinz Eugen,* on 18 May 1941 and was destroyed in battle nine days later.

MEGA FACT
The huge wooden warships of the 18th and 19th centuries were called 'men of war'. Each one carried a crew of up to 800 sailors.

TEXAS TEARAWAY!

The US Navy commissioned its first battleship, USS *Texas,* on 15 April 1895. This coal-burning behemoth had a complement of 30 officers and 362 enlisted crew. She carried two 30cm and six 15cm armaments and also came with four 35cm torpedo tubes. For her time, the USS *Texas* was one of the most powerful battleships in the world.

BISMARCK

In the Battle of Denmark Strait during World War II, the heavy firepower of the great German warship *Bismarck* quickly began to take its toll on the Royal Navy's battlecruisers. In the early hours of 24 May 1941, Lookouts on *Bismarck* spotted two British ships, HMS *Hood* and HMS *Prince of Wales*. Both sides opened fire almost simultaneously. HMS *Hood* was hit in the exchange of fire and started to sink, but the explosion had already killed 95 officers and 1,323 crew. Only three survivors were picked up. *Bismarck* was eventually destroyed by battleships on 27 May 1941, and 2,106 men died.

MEGA CLASS
The 200-year-old *USS Constitution* is the only ship in the US Navy that does not have a classification other than her name. Her reclassification from 'IX-21' to 'None' became effective on 1 September 1975.

DREADNOUGHT

When HMS *Dreadnought* set off on her maiden voyage in 1906, she was the fastest and most heavily armed battleship in the world. While most battleships usually mounted only four big guns, HMS *Dreadnought* carried ten massive 305mm guns. HMS *Dreadnought* was flagship of the Fourth Battle Squadron at the time of the Battle of Jutland in 1916. On 29 March 1915, she rammed and sank the German submarine U-29. HMS *Dreadnought* remains the only battleship to have ever sunk a submarine.

NEW JERSEY

The second *New Jersey* (BB-62) began her career during World War II, where her first action as flagship was a two-day surface and air strike against the Japanese fleet base in the Caroline Islands in the South Pacific. In 1950, *New Jersey* saw active service in the Korean War (1950–1953), and in 1968 she was used as a heavy bombardment ship during the Vietnam War (1954–1975). On 28 December 1982, *New Jersey* was dispatched to Lebanon, where a civil war raged.

MEGA FACT
The last US battleship to see active service was USS Missouri, decommissioned on 31 March 1992.

YAMATO

The Japanese ship *Yamato,* and her sister ship *Musashi,* were the largest battleships ever built. Each one had nine 460mm main battery guns – the largest battleship guns ever to go to sea – and could fire 1460-kilogram armour-piercing shells. *Yamato* was assigned to take part in the suicidal 'Ten-Go' Operation of World War II, which was conceived as a combined air and sea effort to destroy US naval forces supporting the invasion of Okinawa. On 7 April 1945, while still some 320 kilometres north of Okinawa, *Yamato* was attacked and destroyed by a huge force of US carrier planes.

Few modern navies can still afford to build and maintain large surface warships, so there are very few in service. The exceptions are the huge Kirov Class Nuclear-Powered Cruisers (NPCs) of the Russian Navy, which carry a massive amount of weaponry inside a heavily armoured hull.

TICONDEROGA

Twenty-seven Ticonderoga class (CG 47-CG 73) AEGIS guided missile cruisers were built for the US Navy between 1983 and 1994. Four LM-2500 gas turbine engines provide a top speed over 30 knots. The lead ship, USS *Ticonderoga,* comes equipped with two SH-2G Seasprite helicopters for ASW missions. Some of these ships were used during the 1991 Gulf War.

JEANNE D'ARC

Jeanne d'Arc was originally designed as a multi-role helicopter carrier, but she is now a training ship for French Navy cadets during peacetime and an ASW helicopter cruiser with up to eight helicopters in wartime. Carrying two fixed triple launchers for medium-range Exocet MM 38 surface-to-surface missiles (SSMs), *Jeanne d'Arc* can also be deployed as an assault ship and commando carrier for a battalion of up to 700 troops.

KIROV

The most significant large surface warships in service today are the Russian Kirov Class NPCs. The Kirov Class has ten torpedo tubes for 20 Vodopad-NK anti-submarine missiles or torpedoes. These provide the Russian fleet with the capability to engage large surface ships and to defend the fleet against air and submarine attack. Although four Kirov Class NPCs were originally built, only *Admiral Nakhimov*, commissioned in 1988, and *Pyotr Velikhiy*, commissioned in 1995, remain in service.

MEGA RADAR
The radar of the AEGIS Weapons System used in the US Ticonderoga Class automatically detects and tracks air contacts 320 kilometres away.

VITTORIO VENETO

The Italian *Vittorio Veneto* helicopter cruiser was built to pack a punch. The dual-purpose missile launcher could handle both Terrier surface-to-air missiles (SAMs) and Anti-Submarine Rocket (ASROC) missiles. This saved weight and space, and the idea was later adopted by the US Navy. The Terrier missiles were later replaced by the current Standard SM-1ER SAMs. The flight-deck and hangar facilities support up to six Augusta-Bell AB 212 helicopters equipped with search radar and AQS-13B dipping sonar for ASW tasks.

MEGA FACT
Originally a navy's big-gun ship, a 'capital ship' is the term given to the big warship around which a naval fleet is formed.

SMALL WARSHIPS

Many big battleships are capable of carrying a variety of cargo, helicopters, tanks, troops, weapons and even aircraft, but small warships also have their advantages. Smaller vessels can travel through shallow waters and reach areas where bigger warships cannot go. They are also cheaper to build and maintain, and their low weight means they are often very fast through the water.

CLEAN SWEEP

Mines can be dropped by aircraft as well as moored on the water. Mine countermeasure vessels (MCMVs) sweep the surface of the ocean for mines, and many modern MCMVs also come equipped with sonars to detect and locate some very sophisticated and powerful seabed influence mines.

MEGA FACT
The Avenger Class of ships are constructed of wood covered with glass-reinforced plastic (GRP) sheathing, providing some protection against the moored, magnetic and acoustic-influence mines it hunts in the oceans.

LIGHTNING STRIKE

The first torpedo boat was launched by the Royal Navy in 1878. The 19-knot vessel, named *Lightning,* had a torpedo tube in its bow. With the ability to race after much larger ships and sink, or at least severely damage them with its fearsome firepower, *Lightning* was a boat to be taken very seriously by the enemy!

SHIP AHOY!

The Avenger Class ships such as the one shown below are mine countermeasure ships (MCMs) with two electric motors and a hydraulic bow thruster to allow precise positioning and manoeuvring during mine-hunting missions. Despite these ships being some of the largest mine warfare vessels operated by any navy, there is limited room for defensive armament other than two light machine guns.

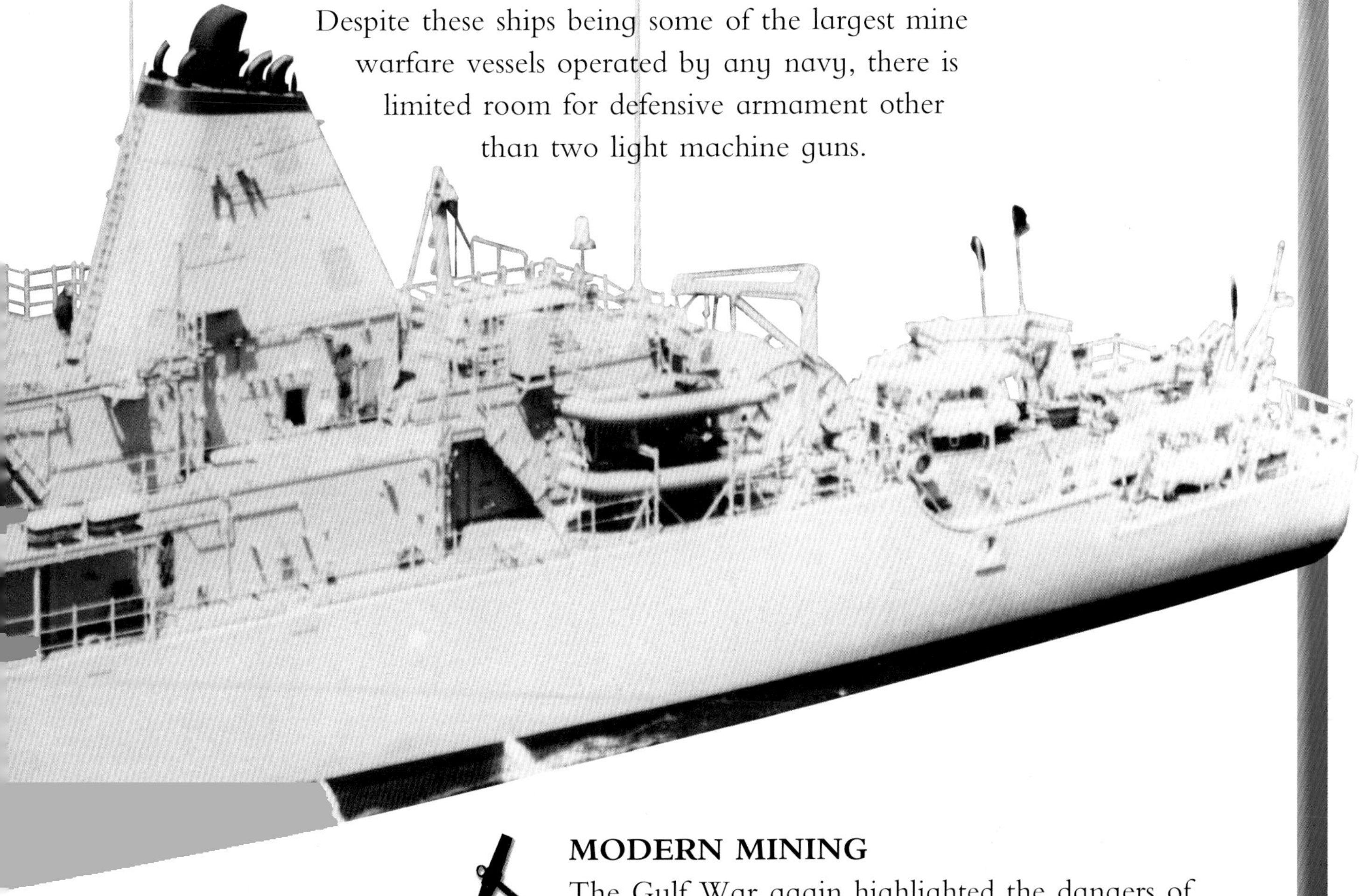

MODERN MINING

The Gulf War again highlighted the dangers of mine warfare with the near catastrophic damage to the USS *Princeton* and the USS *Tripoli* in 1991.

AVENGER

The 12 Avenger MCM vessels in service with the US Navy were commissioned between 1987 and 1994. Each ship accommodates a crew of 80 plus eight officers. This first-of-class vessel was successfully deployed in the Persian Gulf during Operation Desert Storm in 1991. The mine-disposal systems of the Avenger class include the AN/SLQ-37(v) Standard Magnetic/Acoustic Influence Minesweeping System and the EX116 Mod 0 remotely operated vehicle (ROV) mine neutralisation system.

QAHIR CLASS CORVETTES

In 1996, Oman took delivery of two 83m corvettes – the *Qahir Al Amwaj* and *Al Mua'zzar*. These vessels were built in Britain with some unique design features, such as the cladding of the hull and superstructure with radar absorbent material. The corvettes are equipped with two Super Barricade twelve-barrel chaff and infra-red decoy launchers. The *Qahir Al Amwaj* is powered by four medium speed 16 cylinder V form diesel engines, providing 20.7 megawatts of sustained power. The maximum speed of the corvette is 28 knots. The range is 6,400 kilometres at 10 knots and 3,200 kilometres at 20 knots.

MEGA MINES
Some countries clear mines using remotely controlled robotic surface vessels.

FLYVEFISKEN

The Flyvefisken Class multi-role vessels were built for the Royal Danish Navy between 1987 and 1996. Also known as Standard Flex 300 (SF-300), these ships can change role quickly for ASW, MCM, minelaying, pollution control, surface combat or surveillance. The open architecture of the Flyvefisken Class ships allows new weapon systems to be added by creating new nodes. For all roles except pollution control, the ship carries one 76mm OtoBreda Super Rapid gun, which fires 120 rounds per minute with a range of 16 kilometres.

M915 ASTER

The M915 Aster is the Belgian version of a ship better known as the Tripartite. The Belgian Navy launched the first of these mine hunters in 1985 after a long period of development with French and Dutch naval forces. Nine more have since been launched. The M915 Aster clears both moored and bottom mines. Since they all have names of flowers, this class of ships is also known as the 'flower class'. Only the Belgian vessels are designated M915.

AIRCRAFT CARRIERS

Britain had ten aircraft carriers at the beginning of World War II, and the United States had just three. By the end of the war, however, just six years later, the US Navy had increased this fleet to over one hundred vessels. Modern aircraft carriers are giant floating airports, capable of launching a fleet of powerful fighter aircraft and helicopters. Despite their gigantic size, carriers are still vulnerable to submarine attack.

MEGA FACT
In 1911, US pilot Eugene Ely made the first successful flight from a platform rigged on to the deck of a US Navy cruiser.

USS NIMITZ

The Nimitz Class nuclear-powered aircraft carriers are the largest warships ever built. Tasked with a multi-mission attack/ASW role, the first-of-class USS *Nimitz* was commissioned in 1975 and incorporated new technologies such as a multi-function radar system and volume-search radar. The more recent Nimitz Class carriers can reach a speed of over 30 knots. With over 6,000 personnel on board, the carrier has a displacement of 102,000 tonnes and a flight-deck length of 332.9 metres.

MEGA FACT
Decommissioning and disposal costs to inactivate a Nimitz Class nuclear carrier is estimated to be as much as £600 million.

16

USS ENTERPRISE

The USS *Enterprise* was destined to become the world's first nuclear-powered aircraft carrier when the ship was commissioned in 1960. When she was launched a year later, she was also the largest carrier ever built. USS *Enterprise* remains in active service, carrying 100 aircraft with a cruising range the equivalent of almost 20 times around the world. Aircraft carriers play key roles in most modern conflicts. Since they are so large and expensive to build and maintain, however, only major powers, such as the United States, can afford them.

KUZNETSOV CLASS (TYPE 1143.5)

The Kuznetsov Class heavy aircraft-carrying cruisers are the only aircraft carriers in the Russian Navy. These ships support strategic missile-carrying submarines, surface combatants and maritime missile-carrying aircraft. The Klinok air defence missile system provides defence against anti-ship missiles, aircraft and surface ships, and it also comes equipped with anti-ship missile systems with twelve SSM launchers. The *Admiral Kuznetsov* is now the only operational carrier in the Russian fleet.

INVINCIBLE

The first-of-class HMS *Invincible* was commissioned in July 1980 to provide a command headquarters for the task group and support the operations of Vertical/Short Takeoff and Landing (VSTOL) aircraft and helicopters. HMS *Invincible* supports nine Harrier aircraft, nine Sea King HAS 6 ASW helicopters and three Sea King 2 airborne early warning (AEW) helicopters. It has a crew of 740 plus 430 air crew.

DESTROYERS AND FRIGATES

Cruisers, destroyers and frigates are collectively known as surface combatants. They provide a navy with a wide range of capabilities and striking power. Destroyers are usually optimised for anti-aircraft warfare (AAW), deploying a medium or long-range surface-to-air weapons system for area defence. Frigates are generally aimed at ASW. Destroyers are normally larger than frigates, but this distinction has become increasingly blurred as many modern surface combatants combine the two roles.

MEGA FACT

Recent technological advances, such as the AEGIS combat system and the vertical launching system (VLS), have expanded the range of tasks that frigates and destroyers can undertake.

WHAT'S IN A NAME?

Some navies designate larger ships as destroyers, even though they carry only a short-range, point-defence missile system.

IN THE BEGINNING...

Destroyers evolved from a need to counter a new ship that made a devastating debut in the 1891 Chilean Civil War and in the Sino-Japanese War (1894–1895). The new ship was the swift, small torpedo boat, which could draw in close to the larger ships, dispel its torpedoes and make a speedy escape.

MEGA FACT

The US Navy's fleet of destroyers has been evolving since the first ship was commissioned in 1902. The development of the latest Zumwalt Class has continued the trend.

SHIPS FOR THE SHAH

The DDG-993 KIDD Class of multi-purpose destroyers was originally developed by the United States for Iran. The US Navy took the ships back from Iran following the Shah's overthrow by the Muslim cleric Ayatollah Ruhollah Khomeini in 1979. As a result, many military officials refer to these ships as the 'Ayatollah Class'. The KIDD class destroyers are proven ASW and surface-combat vessels with a range of armaments.

KIDD CLASS

The four destroyers that comprise the DDG KIDD Class are the most powerful in the US Navy's fleet. These multi-purpose vessels have proven AAW, ASW and anti-surface warfare (ASU) capabilities. KIDD-Class armaments include the New Threat Upgrade (NTU) AAW system to cope with advances in combat aircraft capabilities, as well as two Mk 26 launchers for standard SAMs. The ships also carry eight Harpoon SSMs, two main guns and a Lamps Mk 1 helicopter. The ship in this picture is the first-of-class USS *Kidd,* commissioned in 1981.

MEGA FACT

The US Knox Class frigate is armed with guns, torpedoes and missiles. It carries a crew of 300 and can speed through the water at 27 knots.

DELHI

With a displacement of 6,700 tonnes, overall length of 163 metres and beam of 17 metres, the Delhi Class destroyers are the Indian Navy's largest warships. The Indian Navy have commissioned four Delhi Class destroyers. The first-of-class INS *Delhi* came in 1997 and is fitted with sophisticated anti-ship, anti-aircraft and anti-submarine sensor and weapon systems. The armament also includes four six-barrel AK 650 gatling guns and four quad launchers for the Uran anti-ship missile system. Two Sea King helicopters provide extra offensive capability.

MEGA FACT
In the 1991 Gulf War, Allied frigates and destroyers conducted deep-strike Tomahawk missile attacks on a range of Iraqi targets.

SOVREMENNY CLASS (TYPE 956)

The Sovremenny Class (Type 956) of destroyers have a typical Russian outfit of offensive weaponry intended for anti-ship warfare, but they are equally adept at anti-air and anti-submarine operations. These ships come with one Ka-25B or Ka-27 helicopter, 48 air-defence missiles, eight anti-ship missiles, torpedoes, mines, long-range guns and a sophisticated electronic-warfare system. The first-of-class Sovremenny destroyer was commissioned in 1985, and another 17 ships have been built for the Russian Navy. Only eight remain in operation.

KONGO

All four Type DDG Kongo Class of guided missile destroyers were built in Japan. *Kongo* was completed in 1993, followed by *Kirishima* in 1995, *Myoukou* in 1996 and *Choukai* in 1998. Plans to build more ships of this class were abandoned due to the high cost of the AEGIS weapons system. These ships are an improved version of the US Arleigh Burke Class (shown below). Some differences include the Kongo's separate fire-control system for the 127mm gun, which has a faster firing rate than the US Navy's Mk 45 127mm gun, a back-up surface/ air search radar and a more sophisticated electronic-warfare system. Kongo's full displacement is larger – 9,300 tonnes to 8,330 tonnes – and it is around 25 metres longer.

MEGA FACT
The US Navy's DDG KIDD Class comprises just four ships — USS Kidd, USS Callaghan, USS Scott and USS Chandler — all commissioned in 1981 and 1982.

TYPE 22 — BROADSWORD

The Royal Navy commissioned a total of 14 Type 22 frigates. The first four ships, commissioned between 1979 and 1982, were *Broadsword*, *Battleaxe*, *Brilliant* and *Brazen*. Some of these frigates saw service in the 1982 Falklands War, where their missile systems proved very effective against Argentine forces. These large vessels were the first Royal Navy ships to be designed without a gun as the main armament. However, Type 22 frigates carry a wide range of armaments, including two fixed quadruple launchers and Seawolf short-range SAM missiles.

LA FAYETTE

The La Fayette Class multi-purpose frigates incorporate a number of stealth features. The sides of the vessel are sloped at 10 degrees to minimise radar cross section, the surfaces are coated in radar-absorbent paint and the profiles of external features have been reduced. These ships are fitted with a fully integrated communications system. The armament includes the 24 VT1 Crotale AAW missile system and the Exocet MM40 SSM. Fourteen units have been ordered by France, Saudi Arabia and Taiwan. Eleven are in service.

DUKE

The Royal Navy's Type 23 Duke Class frigates (HMS *Marlborough* is shown in the picture below) were developed in the 1980s to replace the long-serving Leander Class. A total of 23 ships were planned, but the collapse of the Soviet Union resulted in only 16 being constructed. These frigates incorporate a wide range of weapons, including a single Vickers 114mm gun, four torpedo tubes, Harpoon missiles and Seawolf vertical-launch system (VLS) missiles. Type 23 frigates have played an active role in conflicts in the Falkland Islands, Kosovo, West Africa, and the West Indies.

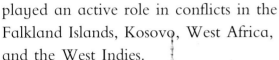

F233

OHP

The Oliver Hazard Perry Class frigates are primarily undersea warfare combatants providing open-ocean escort of convoys in low to medium threat situations. The the end of the Cold War prompted a switch in roles, and the OHP Class now perform tasks as such counter-drug surveillance and interception operations. During the 1991 Gulf War, 14 OHP Class frigates were deployed by the US to the Persian Gulf. The US Navy have 51 OHP Class frigates in operation. Many others have been built for other navies around the world. USS *Crommelin* is shown here.

37

Amphibious missions are one of the most complex of all military operations. They are launched from the sea by naval forces and involve all types of military hardware. The main objective of an amphibious operation is to ensure that landing forces arrive at the destination at the right place and time. Amphibious assault ships use landing craft air cushion (LCAC), conventional landing craft and helicopters to move landing forces ashore. During the 1991 Gulf War, amphibious assault ships dispatched over 18,000 US Marines to the Persian Gulf to support ground troops in Kuwait.

USS ESSEX

The Wasp Class is the first to employ air-cushion landing craft and a squadron of Harrier II (AV-8B) short takeoff and vertical landing (STOVL) jets. The USS *Essex* (LHD 2) was the second of seven Wasp Class ships commissioned by the US Navy. In addition to eight Harriers, these ships also carry assault helicopters for close air support. The armament includes two semi-active radar-guided NATO Seasparrow Missile Systems (NSSMS) for AAW protection and two Phalanx Close-in Weapon-System (CIWS) mounts to counter low-flying aircraft.

MEGA FACT
Construction of the latest Wasp Class amphibious assault ship began in 2003. The US Navy awarded the contract to Northrop Grumman Ship Systems of Mississippi.

HMS OCEAN

HMS *Ocean* was commissioned into the Royal Navy's fleet in 1998. This amphibious helicopter carrier transports 12 Sea King or Merlin helicopters, plus six more Apache, Gazelle or Lynx helicopters. HMS *Ocean* has seen a dramatic start to service. During first-of-class trials, the ship was called to provide humanitarian aid to Honduras following Hurricane Mitch in 1998. Most recently, HMS *Ocean* was used to carry Royal Marines Commandos to Afghanistan.

USS TARAWA

USS *Tarawa* entered service in 1976 to replace the US Navy's helicopter assault carrier and the landing ship dock (LSD). Some 17,000 troops can be carried, along with all their vehicles and equipment. Although these ships are now more than 20 years old, they have been regularly updated. For example, the three 127mm guns fitted as part of the original armament were replaced with an array of modern weapons in 1997/98.

MEGA CREW
HMS Ocean *carries a crew of 255, an air crew of 206 and 480 Royal Marines. An extra 320 marines — all equipped with artillery, vehicles and stores — may be accommodated as a short-term measure.*

ROPUCHA

The strength of the Russian amphibious warfare fleet is the Polish-built Type 775 Ropucha Class. The Russian fleet's amphibious forces have been reduced in recent years, and there are now probably fewer than 12 Ropuchas in service. A typical load for these ships would be 10 main battle tanks (MBTs) with 230 soldiers and an operating crew of 98. All of these ships are beachable, with bow and stern ramps for unloading vehicles.

LOGISTIC SUPPORT VESSELS

Early fighting ships could only stay at sea until ammunition, food, and water needed to be replenished. But modern fleets can stay at sea for months at a time by using a highly organised fleet train to distribute the necessary supplies. Many modern logistic support vessels can dispense supplies in a short time, using sophisticated handling gear for transfer between ships on the move.

MEGA FACT
During World War II, the US Navy perfected a system of keeping ships at sea for long periods by using vessels to replenish ammunition, fuel and other supplies.

MEGA FACT
The Royal Fleet Auxiliary (RFA) is a civilian-crewed fleet owned by the Ministry of Defence (MOD). The main role of the RFA is to supply the Royal Navy with supplies to maintain its operations.

ARGUS

While some navies employ specially designed ships for training purposes, others use converted or modified naval ships that were built for other purposes. The Royal Navy's aviation training ship (ATS) Royal Fleet Auxiliary (RFA) *Argus,* was originally built as the container ship *Contender Bezant.* While the main role of RFA *Argus* was as a helicopter training ship, she was also fitted with an automated combat-information system, enabling her to take part in military operations. In the 1991 Gulf War, RFA *Argus* was used as a hospital ship.

FORT GEORGE

RFA *Fort George* (A388) entered service with her sister ship, RFA *Fort Victoria* (A387), in 1994. Both ships combine the functions of a fleet-support tanker, stores-support ship and helicopter platform. The fuel is pumped through a hose suspended from a cable called a jackstay, which passes to the ship being refuelled. The jackstay can also support a traveller device, carrying loads of up to 2 tonnes.

DURANCE

Five replenishment tankers were built for the French Navy between 1973 and 1990. Four remain in service, but the lead ship – *Durance* – was sold to Argentina in 1999. In addition to the French vessels, a further Durance Class AOR was built in Sydney and commissioned by the Australian Navy as HMAS *Success* in 1986. With a full-load displacement of 17,540 tonnes, the Durance Class armament includes 2 Sinbad twin missile launchers and a Mistral very-short-range SAM.

AMSTERDAM

This combat support ship entered service with the Dutch Navy in 1995. It has two standard replenishment-at-sea (RAS) stations on either beam. The cargo capacity includes 6,680 tonnes of diesel, 1,625 tonnes of aviation fuel and 285 tonnes of stores and provisions. The large hangar can take three medium-sized helicopters. A sister ship called *Patiño* was delivered to the Spanish Navy in 1995.

There are three categories of submarines. Strategic submarines (SSBN) carry long-range ballistic missiles armed with nuclear warheads. Nuclear-powered attack submarine (SSN) operate surveillance missions, communicate tactical information and control the surface and undersea battle space. They also deliver strike weapons or special-operations forces ashore. The third category is a conventional diesel-powered submarine (SSK). The United States and Russia maintain large fleets of strategic submarines, while Britain and France have a smaller number.

MEGA FIRST

The first attack by a submarine was during the American Civil War. The vessel was a semi-submersible steam-propelled vessel called David.

VANGUARD

The SSBN Vanguard Class ballistic missile submarines are the largest submarines made in Britain. They displace 15,900 tonnes of water when submerged – twice that of the Resolution Class Polaris submarines they replaced. These submarines are based at the Royal Naval Base at Faslane, Scotland. The first-of-class HMS *Vanguard* was commissioned in 1993. It has the capacity to carry 16 Trident missiles.

Nuclear Submarines

The limitations of using batteries meant that military scientists soon looked to other sources of power for their fleet of submarines. The development of nuclear technology provided an answer to the problem. Nuclear generators do not need oxygen to work, so a nuclear submarine can stay submerged for weeks at a time. Nuclear submarines are powered by nuclear reactors. These are almost identical to the reactors used in commercial power plants. The reactor produces heat to generate steam, which drives a steam turbine. The turbine shaft in the submarine directly drives the propellers, as well as electrical generators.

SEAWOLF

The SSN Seawolf Class of nuclear-powered submarines was developed to maintain the acoustic advantage of the US fleet over Soviet submarines. The programme was scraped with the end of the Cold War, because it was considered too expensive. Seawolf submarines can accommodate a crew of 134, and they are armed with both the land-attack and an anti-ship version of the Tomahawk missile. The SSN Seawolf Class also have eight 660mm torpedo tubes for torpedo and missile attacks in addition to Boeing's Harpoon anti-ship missiles.

OSCAR

Only two of the Soviet Navy's Type 949 Oscar submarines were ever built, and they entered service between 1982 and 1983. Both have since been decommissioned. The Oscar II was almost identical, except that the hull was 8 metres longer. On 12 August 2000, one of the Oscar II fleet was lost in the Barents Sea following a massive internal explosion. The entire crew – a total of 118 people – died.

AAW
Anti-Air/Aircraft Warfare

AOR
Replenishment Oiler

ASW
Anti-Submarine Warfare

ATS
Aviation Training Ship

CG
Guided Missile Cruiser

CGH
Guided Missile
Helicopter Cruiser

CV
Aircraft Carrier

CVH
Helicopter Carrier

CVS
Aircraft Carrier (Support or ASW)

DDH
Destroyer, Helicopter

DG/DDG
Guided Missile Armed Destroyer

MEGA FACT
*The two-man submarine
was pioneered by the
Italians in World War II.*

FF
Frigate

FFH
Frigate, Helicopter

FG/FFG
Guided Missile Armed Frigate

KNOT
One nautical mile per hour or
1.85 kilometres per hour.

LCAC
Landing Craft, Air-Cushion
(hovercraft)

LCVP
Landing Craft, Vehicle and Personnel

LHA
Amphibious Assault Ship

LPH
Amphibious Assault Ship, Helicopter

LSD
Landing Ship Dock

MCMV
Mine-Countermeasure Vessel

PROPELLER
A shaft, formed in the shape of a spiral, turned by the engine to drive a ship.

RADAR
An instrument that uses radio waves to measure the distance to an object and its speed and direction.

SAM
Surface-to-Air Missile

SONAR
A device that detects the location of an object using sound waves.

SSM
Surface-to-Surface Missile

SSBN
Submarine, Nuclear-Powered, Ballistic Missile Armed

SSG
Submarine, Surface-to-Surface Missile Armed

SSGN
Submarine, Surface-to-Surface Missile Armed, Nuclear-Powered

SSN
Submarine, Nuclear-Powered

STABILISERS
Fins projecting from the side of the hull. Stabilisers help to steady a ship

STOVL
Short Takeoff, Vertical Landing

THRUST
The force that drives ships forward, provided by the turning action of the propellers.

THRUSTERS
Extra propellers in the hull of a ship for moving sideways.

TURBINE ENGINE
High-speed engines that work like jet engines.

VSTOL
Vertical/Short Takeoff and Landing

MEGA FACT
First developed by the United States, the nuclear-powered submarine is the most powerful warship in history.

INDEX

A

Admiral Kuznetsov 17
Admiral Nakhimov 11
AEGIS combat system 11, 18
aircraft carriers 16–17
  light 5
amphibious warfare vessels 24–25
Amsterdam 27
Argus, RFA 26
Avenger Class 13, 14
'Ayatollah Class' 19

B

Battleaxe, HMS 22
battleships 6–9
Bismarck 6, 7, 8
Brazen, HMS 22
Brilliant, HMS 22
Broadsword, HMS 22

C

Callaghan, USS 21
'capital ships' 6, 11
Chandler, USS 21
Choukai 21
Civil War, American 28
Cold War, end 23
Constitution, USS 8
corvettes, Qahir Class 14
Crommelin, USS 23

D

DDG KIDD Class 19, 20, 21
Delhi Class 20
Denmark Strait, Battle of 7
destroyers 18–21
Dreadnought, HMS 8
Duke Class 23
Durance Class 27

E

engines, steam 4

Enterprise, USS 17
Essex, USS 24

F

Falklands War 22
Flyvefisken Class 15
Fort George, RFA 27
Fort Victoria, RFA 27
frigates 18, 20, 22–23

G

Gulf War (1991) 10, 13, 21, 24

H

Hood, HMS 8

I

Invincible, HMS 17

J

jackstays 27
Jeanne d'Arc 10
Jutland, Battle of 5, 8

K

Kidd, USS 20
KIDD Class 19, 20, 21
Kirishima 21
Kirov Class 11
Knox Class 20
Kongo Class 21
Korean War 9
Kuznetsov Class 17

L

La Fayette Class 22
logistic support vessels 26–27

M

M915 Aster 15
'men of war' 7
mine countermeasure (MCM) ships 12,

13, 14, 15
mines
  finding and clearing 12, 14
  production 15
Missouri, USS 9
Myoukou 21

N

New Jersey 9
Nimitz Class 16
nuclear-powered submarines 29

O

Ocean, HMS 25
Oliver Hazard Perry (OHP) Class 22, 23
Osa ships 22
Oscar submarines, Type 949 29

P

Patiño 27
Princeton, USS 13
Pyotr Velikhiy 11

Q

Qahir Class corvettes 14

R

radar-avoidance 22
robotic vessels 14
Romans, ancient 7
Ropucha Class 25
Royal Fleet Auxiliary (RFA) ships 26, 27

S

'S-Boots' 13
Scott, USS 21
Seawolf Class submarines 29
Sovremenny Class 21
Standard Flex 300 (SF-300) 15

stealth features 22
submarines 28–29, 30, 31
supply ships 26, 27
support vessels, logistic 26–27

T

Tarawa, USS 25
'Ten-Go' Operation 9
Texas, USS 7
Ticonderoga class 10, 11
torpedo boats 13
Tripoli, USS 13
triremes 7
Type 22 frigates 22

V

Vanguard Class submarines 28
vertical landing system (VLS) 18
Vietnam War 9
Vittorio Veneto 5, 11

W

warships
  major 10–11
  small 12–14
Wasp Class 24
World War I 5
World War II
  battleships 6, 8, 9
  submarines 30
  supply ships 26
  torpedo boats 13

Y

Yamato 9

Z

Zumwalt Class 19

Military Magazines:

✗ SEA CLASSICS ONLINE
✗ WARSHIPS
✗ Naval History Magazine
✗ PROCEEDINGS

✗ ALL HANDS
✗ Military History
✗ Jane's Defence Weekly

✗ Ships Monthly
✗ Shipping Today & Yesterday
✗ Marine Modelling
✗ Navy International

Picture Credits

Front and back cover top (far left, centre right, far right), TRH; (centre left), MARS; (centre), Leo Van Ginderen; 6/7, MARS; 8 (top), TRH; 8 (bottom), MARS; 9 (both), MARS; 10 (bottom), Leo Van Ginderen; 11 (bottom), MARS; 12/13, MARS; 14 (both), TRH; 15 (bottom), Leo Van Ginderen; 16, MARS; 17 (top), MARS; 17 (centre), TRH; 18/19, MARS; 20 (both), TRH; 21 (bottom), Rex Features; 22 (bottom), TRH; 23 (top), TRH; 24, TRH; 25 (top), TRH; 26, TRH; 27 (all), Leo Van Ginderen. All other pictures Chrysalis Images.